FORWARD

Happy, smiling people make for a better you start the morning off with a joke o your work day, a family-friendly joke helps lighten the mood and gets you thorough a tough day.

The 100 family-friendly jokes in this book are great to share with your family and friends. These are general jokes that have stood the test of time. Comedians and others have rewritten and retold these jokes with their own "flavor". Feel free to tell these jokes with your own personal spin. Look forward to future volumes and be sure to follow us on social media.

A Merry Heart Does Good Like Medicine!

    The Woods Report (YouTube)

    @reportwoods (Twitter)

    woodsreport (Instagram)

    thewoodsreport (Twitch)

JOKE 1

The Great Kangaroo Escape!

A kangaroo kept getting out of his enclosure at the zoo. Knowing that he could hop high, the zoo officials put up a ten-foot fence. He was out the next morning, just sauntering around the zoo.

A twenty-foot fence was put up. Again he got out. When the fence was forty feet high, a camel in the next enclosure asked the kangaroo, "How high do you think they'll go?" The kangaroo said, "Unless somebody locks the gate at night, I think they will just keep going!"

JOKE 2   What's the Worst Age?

"Sixty is the worst age to be," said the 60-year-old man. "You always feel like you have to pee and most of the time you stand there and nothing comes out."

"Ah, that's nothing'," said the 70-year-old. "When you're seventy, you don't have a bowel movement anymore. You take laxatives, eat bran, sit on the toilet all day and nothing' comes out!"

"Actually," said the 80-year-old, "Eighty is the worst age of all." "Do you have trouble peeing, too?" asked the 60-year old. "No, I pee every morning at 6:00. I pee like a racehorse on a flat rock. No problem at all."

"So, do you have a problem with your bowel movement?" "No, I have one every morning at 6:30." Exasperated, the 60-year-old said, "You pee every morning at 6:00 and crap every morning at 6:30. So what's so bad about being 80?"

"I don't wake up until 7:00!!"

JOKE 3

Funeral For My Dog!

Muldoon lived alone in the Irish countryside with only a pet dog for company.

One day the dog died, and Muldoon went to the parish priest and asked, "Father, me dog is dead. Could ya' be saying' a mass for the poor creature?"

Father Patrick replied, "I'm afraid not; we cannot have services for an animal in the church. But there are some Baptists down the lane, an there's no tellin' what they believe. Maybe they'll do something for the creature."

Muldoon said, "I'll go right away Father. Do ya' think $5,000 is enough to donate to them for the service?"

Father Patrick exclaimed, "Sweet Mary and Jesus! Why didn't ya tell me the dog was baptized Catholic?

JOKE 4   Watch Where You Park the Car!

One winter morning while listening to the radio, Bob and his wife hear the announcer say, "We are going to have 4-6 inches of snow today. You must park your car on the even numbered side of the street, so the snowplow can get through."Bob's wife goes out and moves her car.

A week later while they are eating breakfast, the radio announcer says, "We are expecting 6-8 inches of snow today. You must park your car on the odd numbered side of the street, so the snowplow can get through." Bob's wife goes out and moves her car again.

The next week they are having breakfast again, when the radio announcer says, "We are expecting 8-10 inches of snow today. You must park..." then the electric power goes out. Bob's wife is very upset, and with a worried look on her face she says, "Honey, I don't know what to do. Which side of the street do I need to park on so the plow can get through?" With the love and understanding in his voice like all men who are married to blondes exhibit, Bob says, "Why don't you just leave it in the garage this time?"

JOKE 5

Friendship: Male vs Female

Friendship among Women:

A woman didn't come home one night. The next morning she told her husband that she had slept over at a friend's house. The man called his wife's 10 best friends. None of them knew anything about it.

Friendship among Men:

A man didn't come home one night. The next morning he told his wife that he had slept over at a friend's house. The woman called her husband's 10 best friends. Eight confirmed that he had slept over, and two said he was still there.

Men...lol

JOKE 6

From Cradle to Ladle

John invited his mother over for dinner. During the meal his mother couldn't help noticing how beautiful John's roommate was. She had long been suspicious of a relationship between John and his roommate and this only made her more curious. Over the course of the evening, while watching the two interact, she started to wonder if there was more between John and the roommate than met the eye. Reading his mom's thoughts, John volunteered, "I know what you must be thinking, but I assure you, Julie and I are just roommates." About a week later, Julie came to John and said, "Ever since your mother came to dinner, I've been unable to find the beautiful gravy ladle. You don't suppose she took it, do you?" John said, "Well, I doubt it, but I'll write her a letter just to be sure."

So, he sat down and wrote, "Dear Mother, I'm not saying you 'did' take a gravy ladle from my house, and I'm not saying you 'did not' take a gravy ladle. But, the fact remains that one has been missing ever since you were here for dinner."

Several days later, John received a letter from his mother which read: "Dear Son, I'm not saying that you 'do' sleep with Julie, and I'm not saying that you 'do not' sleep with Julie. But, the fact remains that if she was sleeping in her own bed, she would have found the gravy ladle by now. Love, Mom.

Lesson of the day: Don't lie to your mother.

JOKE 7

Child Birthing Advice

During a child birthing class at a local hospital, a nurse says "Ladies, remember that exercise is good for you. Walking is especially beneficial. It strengthens the pelvic muscles and will make delivery that much easier. Just pace yourself, make plenty of stops, and try to stay on a soft surface like grass or a path."

She turns to the men in the room and says "Gentlemen, remember that you're both in this together. It wouldn't hurt for you to go walking with her. In fact, that shared experience would be good for you both."

The room becomes very quiet as the men absorb this information. After a few moments, a man, name unknown, at the back of the room slowly raises his hand. "Yes?" says the Nurse. "I was just wondering if it would be all right if she carries a golf bag while we walk."

JOKE 8

Dear Diary

Her Diary:

Tonight, I thought my husband was acting weird. We had made plans to meet at a nice restaurant for dinner. I was shopping with my friends all day long, so I thought he was upset at the fact that I was a bit late, but he made no comment on it.

Conversation wasn't flowing, so I suggested that we go somewhere quiet so we could talk. He agreed, but he didn't say much. I asked him what was wrong, and he said nothing. I asked him if it was my fault that he was upset. He said he wasn't upset, that it had nothing to do with me, and not to worry about it.

On the way home, I told him that I loved him. He smiled slightly and kept driving. I can't explain his behavior. I don't know why he didn't say, 'I love you too.'

When we got home, I felt as if I had lost him completely, as if he wanted nothing to do with me anymore. He just sat there quietly and watched TV. He continued to seem distant and absent. Finally, with silence all around us, I decided to go to bed. About 15 minutes later, he came to bed. But, I still felt that he was distracted, and his thoughts were somewhere else. He fell asleep – I cried.

I don't know what to do. I am almost sure that his thoughts are with someone else. My life is a disaster.

His Diary:

Motorcycle won't start... can't figure out why.

JOKE 9

Blame it on the Milkman!

A man rushes home and from the door bellows "Guess what heard in the bar today?"

The wife smiles and replies "Some new gossip from you buddies?"

The man nods excitedly and says "They said the milkman has slept with every woman on our block except one." Here he gives his wife a proud smile.

The wife frowns, thinks about it for a moment and replies, "I'l bet it's that stuck-up Phyllis in No. 23. She hates blue colla workers."

JOKE 10 Was It Really A Heart Attack?

A blonde gets home from work early and hears strange noises coming from the bedroom. She rushes upstairs only to find her husband naked lying on the bed, sweating and panting.

"What's going on?" she asks.

"I think I'm having a heart attack," cries the husband.

The blonde rushes downstairs to grab the phone, but just as she's dialing, her four-year-old son comes up and says, "Mommy, Mommy, Aunty Shirley is hiding in the wardrobe, and she has no clothes on."

The blonde slams the phone down and storms back upstairs into the bedroom right past her husband. Rips open the wardrobe door and sure enough, there is her sister, totally naked and cowering on the floor.

"Shirley, how could you?", she screams. "My husband's having a heart attack, and you're hiding in the closet!

JOKE 11

An Honest Game of Golf

Sid and Barney head out for a quick round of golf. Since they are short on time, they decide to play only nine holes.

Sid says to Barney, 'Let's say we make the time worth while, at least for one of us and put $5 on the lowest score for the day.' Barney agrees and they enjoy a great game.

After the eighth hole, Barney is ahead by one stroke but cuts his ball into the rough on the ninth.

'Help me find my ball. You look over there,' he says to Sid. After five minutes, neither has had any luck and since a lost ball carries a four point penalty, Barney pulls a ball from his pocket and tosses it to the ground. 'I've found my ball,' he announces triumphantly.

Sid looks at him forlornly, 'After all the years we've been friends, you'd cheat me on golf for a measly five bucks?'

'What do you mean cheat?' says Barney, 'I found my ball right here.'

'And a liar too,' Sid says with amazement, 'I've been standing on your ball for the last five minutes.'

JOKE 12   The Email From Beyond

A man checked into a hotel. There was a computer in his room, so he decided to send an email to his wife. While typing in her address, he accidentally typed an extra letter and without realizing, sent the email to a widow who just returned from her husband's funeral.

The widow decided to check her email, expecting condolence messages from friends and relatives. After reading the first email she fainted.

Her son rushed in to check on his mother and saw the computer screen with the message:

"To my loving wife. I know you are surprised to hear from me. They have computers here and we are allowed to email our loved ones. I've just been checked in. How are you and the kids? The place is really nice, but I feel lonely without you. I have made necessary arrangements for your arrival tomorrow. I am excited and can't wait to see you."

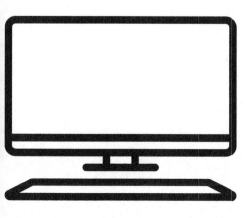

JOKE 13

Super Bowl Tickets!

My brother has 2 tickets for the 2023 SUPER BOWL, both bo.
seats. He paid $2,500 for each ticket, but he didn't realize last
year when he brought them, it was going to be the same day of
his wedding. If you are interested, he is looking for someone to
take his place...

For free...... It's at Shaloh Temple, in Minneapolis at 3pm.

Her name is Brittany McNeill she is 5'1, about 140lbs, good
cook too...She'll be the one in the white dress.

JOKE 14

Wedding Anniversary Gift

Bob was in trouble. He forgot his wedding anniversary. His wife was really pissed.

She told him "Tomorrow morning, I expect to find a gift in the driveway that goes from 0 to 200 in 6 seconds AND IT BETTER BE THERE !!"

The next morning he got up early and left for work. When his wife woke up, she looked out the window and sure enough there was a box gift-wrapped in the middle of the driveway.

Confused, the wife put on her robe and ran out to the driveway, brought the box back in the house.

She opened it and found a brand new bathroom scale.

Bob has been missing since Friday.

JOKE 15

Dishonest Lawer

Murphy, a dishonest lawyer, bribed a man on his client's jury to hold out for a charge of manslaughter, as opposed to the charge of murder which was brought by the state. One carried a penalty of 15 years while the other was a life sentence.

The jury was out for several days before they returned with the manslaughter verdict.

When Murphy paid the corrupt juror, he asked him if he had a very difficult time convincing the other jurors to see things his way.

"Sure did," the juror replied, "the other eleven wanted to acquit."

JOKE 16

New Pastor Visits His Parishioner

A new pastor was visiting his parishioners. At one house it seemed obvious that someone was at home, but no answer came to his repeated knocks at the door. He took out a business card, wrote "Revelation 3:20" on the back of it and stuck it in the door.

When the offering was processed the following Sunday, he found that his card had been returned. Added to it was this cryptic message, "Genesis 3:10."

Reaching for his Bible to check out the citation, he broke up in gales of laughter.

Revelation 3:20 reads: "Behold, I stand at the door and knock."

Genesis 3:10 reads: "I heard your voice in the garden and I was afraid for I was naked."

JOKE 17   Advantages of Mother's Milk

Students in an advanced Biology class were taking their mid-term exam. The last question was, "Name seven advantages of Mother's Milk"? The question was worth 70 points or none at all. One student, in particular, tried to list all seven advantages. He wrote:

1) It is perfect formula for the child.

2) It provides immunity against several diseases.

3) It is always the right temperature.

4) It is inexpensive.

5) It bonds the child to mother, and vice versa.

6) It is always available as needed.

And then the student was stuck. Finally, in desperation, just before the bell rang indicating the end of the test, he wrote:

7) It comes in two attractive containers and it?s high enough off the ground where the cat can?t get it.

JOKE 18

Dave went to his local lotto center to check his ticket. When the clerk checked his ticket Dave was told that he had won 5 million dollars. Dave went right home.

When he saw his wife he said, "I just won the lottery and I am going now to collect my winnings. I want you to be packed before I get back."

His wife very excitedly asked, "What should I pack, warm or cold weather clothes"?

Dave looked at her and said "I don?t care as long as you are gone when I get home."

JOKE 19

A Baptist pastor was presenting a children?s sermon. During the sermon, he asked the children if they knew what the resurrection was.

Now, asking questions during children's sermons is crucial, but at the same time, asking children questions in front of a congregation can also be very dangerous.

Having asked the children if they knew the meaning of the resurrection, a little boy raised his hand. The pastor called on him and the little boy said, "I know that if you have a resurrection that lasts more than four hours you are supposed to call the doctor."

Moral: Don?t let your kids watch too much TV.

JOKE 20   Guy Still Flirts With Dementia

A rather elderly gentleman walks into an upscale hotel cocktail lounge.

He is very well-dressed, smelling slightly of an expensive after-shave, hair well-groomed, great-looking suit, flower in his lapel.

He presents a suave, well-looked-after image.

Seated at the bar is an elderly fine-looking lady in her mid-seventies.

The gentleman walks over, sits down next to her, and orders a drink.

He takes a sip then turns to her and says, "So tell me good looking, do I come here often"?

JOKE 21

A Priest and Nun

A priest and nun are on their way back home from a convention when their car breaks down. They are unable to get repairs completed and it appears that they will have to spend the night in a motel.

The only motel in this town has only one room available so they have a minor problem.

Priest: Sister, I don't think the Lord would have a problem, under the circumstances, if we spent the night together in this one room. I'll sleep on the couch and you take the bed.

Sister: I think that would be okay.

They prepare for bed and each one takes their agreed place in the room. Ten minutes later...

Sister: Father, I'm terribly cold.

Priest: Okay, I'll get up and get you a blanket from the closet.

Ten minutes later...

Sister: Father, I'm still terribly cold.

Priest: Okay Sister, I'll get up and get you another blanket.

Ten minutes later...

Sister: Father, I'm still terribly cold. I don't think the Lord would mind if we acted as man and wife just for this one night.

Priest: You're probably right...get up and get your own blanket!

JOKE 22

Wake Me Up Before You Go!

Man and his wife were having some problems at home and were giving each other the silent treatment.

Suddenly, the man realized that the next day, he would need his wife to wake him up at 5:00am for an early morning business flight.

Not wanting to be the first to break the silence (and **LOSE**), he wrote on a piece of paper:

"Please wake me at 5:00 am" he left it where he knew she would find it.

The next morning, the man woke up, only to discover it was 9 am and he missed his flight.

Furious, he was about to go find out why his wife hadn't wakened him, when he noticed a piece of paper by the bed. The paper said, "it's 5am. Wake up".

JOKE 23

Dr. Geezer's Clinic

An old geezer became very bored in retirement and decided to open a medical clinic. He put a sign up outside that said, "Dr. Geezer's clinic. Get your treatment for $500. If not cured, get back $1,000."

Doctor "Young," who was positive that this old geezer didn't know beans about medicine, thought this would be a great opportunity to get $1,000. So he went to Dr. Geezer's clinic. This is what transpired:

Dr. Young: "Dr. Geezer, I have lost all taste in my mouth. Can you please help me?"

Dr. Geezer: "Nurse, please bring medicine from box 22 and put 3 drops in Dr. Young's mouth."

Dr. Young: "Yuck, this is gasoline!"

Dr. Geezer: "Congratulations! You've got your taste back. That will be $500."

Dr. Young gets annoyed and goes back after a couple of days, figuring to recover his money.

Dr. Young: "I have lost my memory; I can not remember anything."

Dr. Geezer: "Nurse, please bring medicine from box 22 and put 3 drops in the patient's mouth."

Dr. Young: "No, last time that was gasoline!"

Dr. Geezer: "Congratulations! You've got your memory back. That will be $500."

Dr. Young (after having lost $1000) leaves angrily and comes back after several more days.

Dr. Young: "My eyesight has become weak; I can hardly see anything!"

Dr. Geezer: "Well, I don't have any medicine for that, so here's your $1000 back." (giving him a $10 bill)

Dr. Young: "But this is only $10!"

Dr. Geezer: "Congratulations! You got your vision back! That will be $500."

Moral of story– Just because you're "Young" doesn't mean that you can outsmart an "Old Geezer"

JOKE 24

The Neighbor's Visit

A farmer drove to a neighbor's farmhouse and knocked at the door. A boy, about 9, opened the door.

"Is your dad or mom home?" said the farmer.

"No, they went to town."

"How about your brother, Howard? Is he here?"

"No, he went with Mom and Dad."

The farmer stood there for a few minutes, shifting from one foot to the other, and mumbling to himself.

"I know where all the tools are, if you want to borrow one, or I can give Dad a message."

"Well," said the farmer uncomfortably, "I really wanted to talk to your Dad. It's about your brother Howard getting my daughter Suzy pregnant!!"

The boy thought for a moment.

"You would have to talk to Dad about that. I know he charges $500 for the bull and $50 for the boar, but I don't know how much he charges for Howard."

JOKE 25

A husband told his wife, "From now on, you need to know that am the man of this house. You will prepare me dinner and dessert. After dinner, you will go upstairs with me and well you get the point. You will draw me a bath. You will wash my back dry me, and bring me my robe... You will massage my feet and hands. Tomorrow, guess who's going to dress me and comb m hair?" wife replied, "The funeral director."

JOKE 26

Job Opening At The Zoo

A man is desperate for a job and finds himself at the zoo. The manager tells him there's only one job opening but he has to promise not to tell anyone about it. The man agrees, and so the manager whispers to him: "Ever since jumbo, the chimp died, this zoo's hardly having visitors. So what I want you to do is dress up in this chimpanzee costume and entertain the guests. What do you say? I'll pay you $50 an hour?"

The man thinks long and hard and thinks what the heck, he needs a job really bad, and this one pays pretty good. So the man is starting to enjoy his job, doing tricks on the monkey bars to wow the guests. One day on the monkey wires, he slips and falls right into the lions exhibit. The lion starts to bare its teeth and growl.

Frightened, the man starts screaming for help when the lion jumps on him and whispers in his ear: "SHUT UP or you'll get us both fired!"

JOKE 27

A teacher asks her class, "What do you want to be when you grow up?

Little Johnny says "I wanna be a billionaire, go to the most expensive clubs, take the hottest girl with me, give her a Ferrari, an apartment in Hawaii, a mansion in Paris, a jet to travel through Europe, and have an Infinite Visa Card.

The teacher, shocked, and not knowing what to do with the bad behavior of the child, decides not to give importance to what he said and then continues the lesson.

"And you, Susie?" the teacher asks.

Susie says "I wanna be with Johnny.

JOKE 28

Tie A Ribbon On It!

This couple has a dog that snored. Annoyed because she can't sleep, the wife goes to the vet to see if he could help. The vet tells the woman to tie a ribbon around the dog's testicles, and he will stop snoring. "Yeah, right!" she says and walks away.

The wife tosses and turns, unable to sleep. Muttering to herself, she goes to the closet and grabs a piece of red ribbon and ties it carefully around the dog's testicles. Sure enough, the dog stops snoring. The woman is amazed and falls asleep happy.

Later that night, her husband returns home drunk from being out drinking with his buddies. He climbs into bed, falls asleep and immediately begins snoring loudly.

Awaken, the woman decides maybe the ribbon might work on him. So, she goes to the closet again, grabs a piece of blue ribbon and ties it around her husband's testicles. Amazingly, it also works on him. The woman falls asleep and sleeps soundly.

The husband wakes from his drunken stupor and stumbles into the bathroom. As he stands in front of the toilet, he glances in the mirror and sees a blue ribbon attached to his privates. He is very confused, and as he walks back into the bedroom, he sees the red ribbon attached to his dog's testicles.

He shakes his head, looks at the dog and whispers, "Buddy, I don't know where we were or what we did last night, but we took first and second place!"

JOKE 29

Bill and Bob, two ten year olds, were sitting in the waiting room of a pediatric clinic. Bill happened to be crying very loudly.

"Why are you crying?" Bob asked.

"I came here for a blood test," sobbed Bill.

"So? Are you afraid?"

"No. For the blood test, but mom said they will cut my finger to get the blood."

As Bob heard this, he immediately began crying profusely.

Astonished, Bill stopped his tears and asked Bob, "And why are you crying now?"

To which Bob replied, "Mom brought me for a urine test!"

It was three o'clock in the morning, and the receptionist at a posh hotel was just dozing off, when a little old lady came running towards her, screaming.

"Please come quickly!" she yelled, "I just saw a naked man outside my window!" The receptionist immediately rushed up to the old lady's room.

"Where is he?" asked the receptionist.

"He's over there," replied the little old lady, pointing to an apartment building opposite the hotel.

The receptionist looked over and could see a man with no shirt on, moving around his apartment.

"It's probably a man who's getting ready to go to bed," she said reassuringly. "And how do you know he's naked, you can only see him from the waist up?"

"The dresser, honey!" screamed the old lady. "Try standing on the dresser!"

JOKE 31

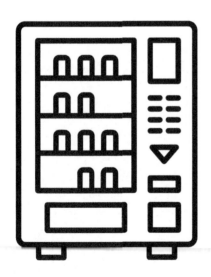

The Soda Machine

A blonde was standing in front of a soda machine outside of a local store. After putting in sixty cents, a root beer popped out of the machine.

She set it on the ground, put sixty more cents into the machine, and pushed another button. A can of coke come out of the machine.

She continued to do this until a man standing behind her and waiting to use the machine became impatient.

"Excuse me, can I get my soda and then you can go back to whatever stupid thing you are doing?" he asked.

The blonde turned around and said, "Yeah right! I'm not giving up this machine while I'm still winning!"

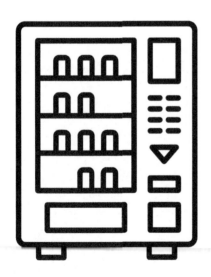

JOKE 32

The Final Will

When Jim retired, he and his wife, who was much, much younger, moved to a beach town.

Once they'd settled in, he decided it was about time to make a will, so he made an appointment with a lawyer.

"I want it to be nice and straightforward," he instructed the attorney, "Everything goes to my wife: the house, the car, the pension and the life insurance, under one condition that she remarry within the year."

"Fine, Mr. Ramsey," said the lawyer, "But do you mind my asking why the condition?"

"Simple! I want at least one person to be sorry I died."

JOKE 33

Once upon time a four-year-old boy was visiting his aunt and uncle and staying over while his parents went on a vacation. He was a very outspoken little boy and often had to be censured to say the right thing at the right time.

One day at lunch, when the aunt had company, the little boy said, "Auntie, I want to tinkle." Auntie took the little boy aside and said, "Never say that, sonny. If you want to tinkle, say, 'I want to whisper.'" And the incident was forgotten.

That night at when Uncle and Auntie were soundly sleeping, the little boy climbed into bed with them. He tugged at his uncle's shoulder and said, "Uncle, I want to whisper." Uncle said, "All right, sonny, just don't wake Auntie up. Whisper in my ear." So the little boy did.

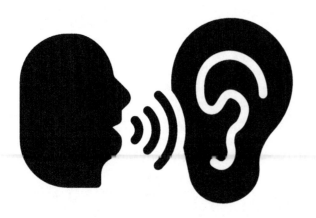

JOKE 34

Walking Is Beneficial

During a child birthing class at a local hospital, a nurse says, "Ladies, remember that exercise is good for you. Walking is especially beneficial. It strengthens the pelvic muscles and will make delivery that much easier. Just pace yourself, make plenty of stops and try to stay on a soft surface like grass or a path."

She turns to the men in the room and says "Gentlemen, remember that you're both in this together. It wouldn't hurt for you to go walking with her. In fact, that shared experience would be good for you both."

The room becomes very quiet as the men absorb this information. After a few moments a man, name unknown, at the back of the room slowly raises his hand. "Yes?" says the Nurse. "I was just wondering if it would be all right if she carries a golf bag while we walk."

JOKE 35

It was the end of the school year, and a kindergarten teacher was receiving gifts from her pupils.

The florist's son handed her a gift. She shook it, held it overhead, and said, "I bet I know what it is. Flowers."

"That's right," the boy said, "but how did you know?"

"Oh, just a wild guess," she said.

The next pupil was the sweet shop owner's daughter. The teacher held her gift overhead, shook it, and said, "I bet I can guess what it is. A box of sweets."

"That's right, but how did you know?" asked the girl.

"Oh, just a wild guess," said the teacher.

The next gift was from the son of the liquor store owner. The teacher held the package overhead, but it was leaking. She touched a drop off the leakage with her finger and put it to her tongue.

"Is it wine?" she asked.

"No," the boy replied, with some excitement.

The teacher repeated the process, tasting a larger drop of the leakage.

"Is it champagne?" she asked.

"No," the boy replied, with more excitement.

The teacher took one more big taste before declaring, "I give up, what is it?"

With great glee, the boy replied, "It's a puppy!"

JOKE 36

The Old Couple's Meal

An older couple entered a burger joint. The old man placed an order for one hamburger, french fries, and a drink.

When the food arrived, he unwrapped the plain hamburger and carefully cut it in half, placing one half in front of his wife. He then carefully counted out the french fries, dividing them into two piles, and neatly placed one pile in front of his wife. He took a sip of the drink, his wife took a sip, and then they set the cup down between them.

As he began to eat his few bites of hamburger, the people around them were looking over and whispering. Obviously, they were thinking, "That poor old couple—all they can afford is one meal for the two of them."

As the man began to eat his fries, a young man came to the table and politely offered to buy another meal for the old couple. The old man said they were just fine; they were used to sharing everything.

People closer to the table noticed the little old lady hadn't eaten a bite. She sat there watching her husband eat and occasionally taking turns sipping the drink.

Again, the young man came over and begged them to let him buy another meal for them. This time, the old woman said, "No, thank you; we are used to sharing everything."

Finally, as the old man finished and was wiping his face neatly with the napkin, the young man again came over to the little old lady who had yet to eat a single bite of food and asked "What is it you are waiting for?"

She answered, "The teeth."

JOKE 37

This past spring semester at Duke University, there were two sophomores who were taking organic chemistry and who did pretty well on all of the quizzes, midterms, labs, etc. Going into the final exam, they had solid As.

These two friends were so confident going into the final that the weekend before finals week (even though the chemistry final was on Monday) they decided to go up to the University of Virginia for a party with some friends.

So they did this and had a great time. However, they ended up staying longer than they planned, and they didn't make it back to Duke until early Monday morning. Rather than taking the final then, they found Professor Aldric after the final and explained to him why they missed it. They told him that they went up to Virginia for the weekend and had planned to come back in time to study, but that they had a flat tire on the way back, didn't have a spare, and couldn't get help for a long time. So they were late getting back to campus.

Aldric thought this over and agreed that they could make up the final the following day. The two guys were elated and relieved. So they studied that night and went in the next day at the time that Aldric had told them.

He placed them in separate rooms, handed each of them a test booklet, and told them to begin. They looked at the first problem, which was something simple about free radical formation and was worth 5 points. "Cool," they thought, "this is going to be easy." They solved that problem and then turned the page.

The next page featured one question worth 95 points: "Which tire?"

JOKE 38
Girls Getaway

Four friends spend weeks planning the perfect girls getaway trip, shopping, casinos, massages, facials.

Two days before the group is to leave Mary's husband puts his foot down and tells her she isn't going.

Mary's friends are very upset that she can't go, but what can they do.

Two days later the three get to the hotel only to find Mary sitting in the bar drinking a glass of wine.

"Wow, how long you been here and how did you talk your husband into letting you go?"

"Well, I've been here since last night... Yesterday evening I was sitting on the couch and my husband came up behind me and put his hands over my eyes and said 'Guess who'?"

I pulled his hands off to find all he was wearing was his birthday suit. He took my hand and lead me to our bedroom. The room was scented with perfume, had two dozen candles and rose petals all over... On the bed, he had handcuffs and ropes! He told me to tie and cuff him to the bed, so I did. And then he said, "Now, you can do whatever you want.

So....here I am."

JOKE 39

Which Room in Hell?

Three men went to hell.

The devil said to them "You have come to hell, and you must now choose whether to spend eternity in room 1, 2 or 3"

He then opened the doors to the three rooms.

Room 1 was filled with men standing on their heads, on a hard wooden floor.

Room 2 was filled with men standing on the heads, on a cement floor.

Finally, room 3 had just a few men, standing in boo boo up to their knees and drinking coffee.

The men thought for a while, and decided to go with room 3, as it was less crowded and they could drink coffee.

They entered the door to room 3 and just as it was closing behind them, the devil said "OK men, coffee break's over. Back on your heads."

The Christmas List to Jesus

A mafioso's son sits at his desk writing a Christmas wish list to Jesus.

He first writes, 'Dear baby Jesus, I have been a good boy the whole year, so I want a new...' He looks at it, then crumples it up into a ball and throws it away.

He gets out a new piece of paper and writes again, 'Dear baby Jesus, I have been a good boy for most of the year, so I want a new...' He again looks at it with disgust and throws it away.
He then gets an idea.

He goes into his mother's room, takes a statue of the Virgin Mary, puts it in the closet, and locks the door.

He takes another piece of paper and writes, 'Dear baby Jesus. If you ever want to see your mother again...'

JOKE 41

A lawyer was cross-examining the doctor about whether or no he had checked the pulse of the deceased before he signed th death certificate.

"No," the doctor said. "I did not check his pulse."

"And did you listen for a heartbeat?" asked the lawyer.

"No I did not," the doctor said.

"So," said the lawyer, "when you signed the death certificate you had not taken steps to make sure he was dead."

The doctor said, "Well, let me put it this way. The man's brai was in a jar on my desk but, for all I know, he could be ou practicing law somewhere."

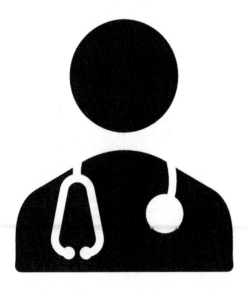

JOKE 42

Locker Room Surprise!

Smith and Jones were playing racquetball in the local gym.

After the game, they went into the locker room to change, and Smith is shocked and amazed to see Jones wearing a lace bra and garter belt.

Smith: "My God, Jones, when did you start wearing women's underwear?"

Jones: "Ever since my wife found them in the glove compartment of my car!"

JOKE 43   No Fishing on the Lake

One morning, a husband returns the family boat to their lakeside cottage after several hours of fishing and decides to take a nap. Although not familiar with the lake, the wife decides to take the boat out. She motors out a short distance, anchors, puts her feet up and begins to read her book. The peace and solitude are magnificent.

Along comes a Fish and Game Warden in his boat. He pulls up alongside the woman and says, "Good morning, Ma'am. What are you doing?"

"Reading a book," she replies, thinking, "Isn't that obvious?"

"You're in a Restricted Fishing Area," he informs her.

"I'm sorry, officer, but I'm not fishing. I'm reading."

"Yes, but I see you have all the equipment. For all I know you could start at any moment. I'll have to take you in and write you up."

"If you do that, I'll have to charge you with sexual assault," says the woman.

"But I haven't even touched you," says the Game Warden.

"That's true, but you have all the equipment. For all I know you could start at any moment."

"Have a nice day ma'am," and he left.

The Woods Report

 **44**   **History Paper Update**

At dinner, a father is asking his kids about the school. He turns to the oldest daughter "How is your history paper coming along, dear?"

"Well, it was hard at first. My history professor suggested that I use the internet for research and it's been very helpful."

Surprised at the professor's suggestion, the father asked "Oh really, how so?"

"Yes, so far I've located 7 people who will write it and sell it to me for a good price."

JOKE 45

Broken Lawn Mower

When our lawn mower broke and wouldn't run, my wife kept hinting to me that I should get it fixed. But, somehow I always had something else to take care of first, the shed, the boat, making beer. Always something more important to me.

Finally she thought of a clever way to make her point. When I arrived home one day, I found her seated in the tall grass, busily snipping away with a tiny pair of sewing scissors.

I watched silently for a short time and then went into the house. I was gone only a minute, and when I came out again I handed her a toothbrush.

I said, "When you finish cutting the grass, you might as well sweep the driveway."

The doctors say I will walk again, but I will always have a limp.

JOKE 46 — Good News and Bad News

A man was hunting when a gust of wind blew, the gun fell over & discharged, shooting him in the genitals.

Several hours later, lying in a hospital bed, he was approached by his doctor.

"Well, sir, I have some good news & some bad news. The good news is that you are going to be OK. The damage was local to your groin, there was very little internal damage, and we were able to remove all of the buckshot."

"What's the bad news?" asked the hunter.

"The bad news is that there was some pretty extensive buckshot damage done to your willy which left quite a few holes in it. I'm going to have to refer you to my sister."

"Well, I guess that isn't too bad," the hunter replied. "Is your sister a plastic surgeon?"

"Not exactly," answered the doctor. "She's a flute player in the Boston Symphony Orchestra. She's going to teach you where to put your fingers so you don't pee in your eye."

JOKE 47

The Truck Driver

A guy driving a pickup truck in the middle of nowhere picks up a hitch-hiker. It gets dark and the hitch-hiker falls asleep. Suddenly bang, and the hitch-hiker wakes up.

"What the hell was that?" he asks shaken.

The truck driver replies, "Ehh, just some kinda animal, go back to sleep."

Further the same thing again, bang, "What the hell was that?"

"some kinda animal again."

Further into the night, the hitch-hiker wakes up to bang, bang, bang.

"What the hell was that?"

"One of my wife's lovers!"

"How terrible," says the hitch-hiker, "but there were 3 bangs."

The truck driver replies, "Yeah, well I had to go through two fences to get the him!"

JOKE 48   5 Whiskey Shots

A man goes into a bar and seats himself on a stool. The bartender looks at him and says, "What'll it be buddy?"

The man says, "Set me up with five whiskey shots, and make 'em doubles."

The bartender does this and watches the man slug one down, then the next, then the next, and so on until all five are gone almost as quickly as they were served.

Staring in disbelief, the bartender asks why he's doin' all this drinking.

"You'd drink 'em this fast too if you had what I have."
The bartender hastily asks, "What do you have pal?"
The man quickly replies, "I only have a dollar."

JOKE 49   Boneless Chicken Breasts

A supermarket had a sale on boneless chicken breasts, and a woman intended to stock up. At the store, however, she was disappointed to find only a few skimpy pre-packaged portions of the poultry, so she complained to the butcher in a rather mean and arrogant manner.

"Don't worry," he said. "I'll pack some more trays and have them ready for you by the time you finish shopping."

Several aisles later, the butcher's voice came booming over the speaker system, "Will the lady who wanted bigger breasts please meet me at the back of the store."

JOKE 50   Sooo Much In Common

Two men were sitting next to each other at Murphy's Pub in London. After awhile, one man looks at the other and says, 'I can't help but think, from listening to you, that you're from Ireland' The other man responds proudly, 'Yes, that I am!' The first one says, 'So am I!

And where about from Ireland might you be?' The other man answers, 'I'm from Dublin, I am.' The first one responds, 'So am I!' 'Mother Mary and begora.

And what street did you live on in Dublin?' The other man says, 'A lovely little area it was. I lived on McCleary Street in the old central part of town.' The first one says, 'Faith and it's a small world. So did I! So did I!

And to what school would you have been going?' The other man answers, 'Well now, I went to St. Mary's, of course.' The first one gets really excited and says, 'And so did I.

Tell me, what year did you graduate?' The other man answers, 'Well, now, let's see. I graduated in 1964.' The first one exclaims, 'The Good Lord must be smiling down upon us! I can hardly believe our good luck at winding up in the same place tonight. Can you believe it, I graduated from St. Mary's in 1964 my own self!'

About this time, Vicky walks up to the bar, sits down and orders a drink.

Brian, the barman, walks over to Vicky, shaking his head and mutters, 'It's going to be a long night tonight.'

Vicky asks, 'Why do you say that, Brian?'

The Murphy twins are drunk again.'

JOKE 51

Late Night Lecture

An elderly man is stopped by the police around 2 A.M. and is asked where he is going at this time of night. The man replies, "I am on my way to a lecture about alcohol abuse and the effects it has on the human body, as well as smoking and staying out late." The officer then asks, "Really? Who is giving that lecture at this time of night?" The man replies, "That would be my wife."

JOKE 52   Gone for Days

Roger left for work on Friday morning. Friday was payday, so instead of going home, he stayed out the entire weekend partying with the boys and spending his entire pay packet.

Finally, Roger appeared at home on Sunday night, and obviously he was confronted by his angry wife, Martha who lectured Roger for nearly two hours with a tirade befitting his actions. Finally, Martha stopped the nagging and said to Roger, 'How would you like it if you didn't see me for two or three days?'

Roger replied grimly, 'That would be fine with me.'

Monday went by and he didn't see his Martha. Tuesday and Wednesday came and went with the same results.

By the Thursday, the swelling had gone down just enough so that Roger he could see Martha a little out of the corner of his left eye

JOKE 53

Golfing Lessons

Four men waited at the men's tee while four women were hitting in front of them, taking their time.

When the final lady was ready to hit her ball, she hacked it 10 feet. Then she went over and missed it completely. Then she hacked it another ten feet and finally hacked it another five feet

She looked up at the patiently waiting men and trying to be cool about her bad game said, "I guess all those f***ing lessons took over the winter didn't help."

One of the men immediately responded, "Well, there you have it. You should have taken golf lessons instead!"

JOKE 54   The Guitarist

As a guitarist, I play many gigs. Recently, I was asked by a funeral director to play at a graveside service for a poor, humble man. The service was to be at a pauper's cemetery in the back country. As I was not familiar with that area, I got lost.

I finally arrived an hour late and saw the funeral guy had evidently gone, and the hearse was nowhere in sight. There were only the diggers and crew left, and they were eating lunch.

I felt badly and apologized to the men for being late. I went to the side of the grave and looked down, and the vault lid was already in place. I didn't know what else to do, so I started to play.

The workers put down their lunches and began to gather around. I played out my heart and soul for this man with no family and friends. I played like I've never played before for this homeless man.

And as I played 'Amazing Grace,' the workers began to weep. They wept, I wept, and we all wept together. When I finished, I packed up my guitar and started for my car. Though my head hung low, my heart was full.

As I opened the door to my car, I heard one of the workers say, "I've never seen anything like that before, and I've been putting in septic tanks for twenty years."

JOKE 55

The Lion Tamer

Two unemployed guys are talking. One says, "I'm going to become a lion tamer."

The other replies, "That's crazy, you don't know nothing about no lion taming."

"I can figure it out!"

"Well, OK, answer me this. When one of those lions comes at you a roaring and biting, what you gonna do?"

"Well, then I take that big chair they all carry, and I stick it in his face until he backs down."

"Well, what if the lion takes that big paw, and hooks the chair with them big claws, and throws that chair out of the cage? What do you do then?"

"Well, then I takes that whip they all carry, and I whip him and whip him until he backs down."

"Well, what if that lion bites that whip with his big teeth, and bites it two? What you gonna do then?"

"Well, then I take that gun they all carry, and I shoot him."

"Well, what if that gun doesn't work? What will you do then?"

"Well, then I pick up some of the crap that's on the bottom of the cage and I throw it in his eyes, and I run out of the cage."

"Well, what if there ain't no crap on the bottom of the cage? What you gonna do then?"

"Well, that's dumb. If that lion comes at me, and he throws the chair out of the cage, and he bites the whip in two, and my gun don't work there's going to be some crap on the bottom of that cage, you can bet on that."

JOKE 56

Three Old Ladies

Three old ladies were discussing the trials and tribulations of getting older.

One said, "Sometimes I catch myself with a jar of mayonnaise in my hand while standing in front of the refrigerator, and I can't remember whether I need to put it away or start making a sandwich."

The second lady chimed in with, "Yes, sometimes I find myself on the landing of the stairs and can't remember whether I was on my way up or on my way down."

The third one responded, "Well, ladies, I'm glad I don't have that problem, knock on wood," as she rapped her knuckles on the table and then said, "That must be the door, I'll get it!"

JOKE 57

The Rude Parrot

A young man named John received a parrot as a gift. The parrot had a bad attitude and an even worse vocabulary. Every word out of the bird's mouth was rude, obnoxious and laced with profanity.

John tried and tried to change the bird's attitude by consistently saying only polite words, playing soft music and anything else he could think of to 'clean up' the bird's vocabulary.

Finally, John was fed up and he yelled at the parrot. The parrot yelled back. John shook the parrot and the parrot got angrier and even more rude. John, in desperation, threw up his hand, grabbed the bird and put him in the freezer.

For a few minutes the parrot squawked and kicked and screamed. Then suddenly there was total quiet. Not a peep was heard for over a minute. Fearing that he'd hurt the parrot, John quickly opened the door to the freezer. The parrot calmly stepped out onto John's outstretched arms and said "I believe I may have offended you with my rude language and actions. I'm sincerely remorseful for my inappropriate transgressions and I fully intend to do everything I can to correct my rude and unforgivable behavior."

John was stunned at the change in the bird's attitude. As he was about to ask the parrot what had made such a dramatic change in his behavior, the bird spoke-up, very softly, "May I ask what the turkey did?"

JOKE 58   The Red Stoplight

Two elderly women were out driving in a large car. Both could barely see over the dashboard. As they were cruising along, they came to an intersection. The stoplight was red, but they just went on through. The woman in the passenger seat thought to herself, "I must be losing it. I could have sworn we just went through a red light." After a few more minutes, they came to another intersection, and the light was red again. They went right though it. This time, the woman in the passenger seat was almost sure that the light had been red and was really concerned that she was losing it. She was getting nervous and decided to pay very close attention to the road and the next intersection to see what was going on. At the next intersection, the light was definitely red, and sure enough, they went right through again. She turned to the other woman and said, "Mildred! Did you know we just ran through three red lights in a row? You could have killed us!" Mildred turned to her and said, "Oh my, am I driving?"

JOKE 59

Broken Window

Joe's dad scolded him for breaking the neighbor's window with a baseball.

"What did he say to you when you broke his window?" asked the father.

"Do you want to hear what he said with or without the bad words?"

"Without, of course."

"Well, then, he said nothing."

JOKE 60

Change Your Course

Through the pitch-black night, the captain sees a light dead ahead on a collision course with his ship. He sends a signal: "Change your course 10 degree east."

The light signals back: "Change yours, 10 degrees west."

Angry, the captain sends: "I'm a navy captain! Change your course, sir!"

"I'm a seaman, second class," comes the reply. "Change your course, sir."

Now the captain is furious. "I'm in a battleship! I'm not changing course!"

There is one last reply. "I'm in a lighthouse. Your call."

JOKE 61

The Hunting Contest

A blonde, a brunette, and a redhead all entered a hunting contest. Th[e] winner could win $500.

The redhead went out, found some tracks, followed the tracks, an[d] came back with a 250 pound bear.

Then the brunette went out, found some tracks, followed the track[s] and came back with a 275 pound buck.

Finally, the blonde had to beat 275lbs, so she went out and foun[d] some tracks. She followed the tracks and came back with a broke[n] leg and an arm, no teeth and blood all over.

The judge asked "What happened????"

The blonde said "I found some tracks, followed the tracks, and got h[it] by a train."

JOKE 62

Lifesavers As A Treat

A grade school teacher often gave her students Lifesavers as a treat.

The children began to identify the flavors by their color:

Red....................Cherry
Yellow................Lemon
Green.................Lime
Purple ....Grape

Finally the teacher gave them all honey lifesavers. None of the children could identify the taste.

The teacher said, "I will give you all a clue. It's what your Mother may sometimes call your father."

One little girl looked up in horror, spit her lifesaver out and yelled, "Oh my God! They're a-holes!"

JOKE 63

The Truck Driver's Delima

A truck driver was driving along on the freeway. A sign came up that read, "Low bridge ahead."

Before he knew it, the bridge was right ahead of him, and he got stuck under it. Cars backed up for miles.

Finally, a police car came up. The cop got out of his car and walked around to the truck driver. He put his hands on his hips and said with a smirk, "Got stuck, huh?"

The annoyed truck driver replied, "No, I was delivering this bridge and ran out of gas."

JOKE 64

Questions for God ??

Little Jimmy was laying about on a hillock in the middle of a meadow on a warm spring day. Puffy white clouds rolled by and he pondered their shape. Soon, he began to think about God. "God? Are you really there?" Jimmy said out loud.

To his astonishment a voice came from the clouds. "Yes, Jimmy? What can I do for you?"

Seizing the opportunity, Jimmy asked, "God? What is a million years like to you?"

Knowing that Jimmy could not understand the concept of infinity, God responded in a manner to which Jimmy could relate. "A million years to me, Jimmy, is like a minute."

"Oh," said Jimmy. "Well, then, what's a million dollars like to you?"

"A million dollars to me, Jimmy, is like a penny."
"Wow!" remarked Jimmy, getting an idea. "You're so generous. Can I have one of your pennies?"

God replied, "Sure thing, Jimmy! Just a minute."

JOKE 65

A Hole In One!

Reverend Francis Norton woke up Sunday morning and, realizing it was an exceptionally beautiful and sunny early spring day, decided he just had to play golf. So he told the Associate Pastor that he was feeling sick and convinced him to lead Mass for him that day.

As soon as the Associate Pastor left the room, Father Norton headed out of town to a golf course about forty miles away. This way he knew he wouldn't accidentally meet anyone he knew from his parish. Setting up on the first tee, he was alone. After all, it was Sunday morning and everyone else was in church!

At about this time, Saint Peter leaned over to the Lord while looking down from the heavens and exclaimed, "You're not going to let him get away with this, are you?"

The Lord sighed, and said, "No, I guess not."
Just then Father Norton hit the ball and it shot straight towards the pin, dropping just short of it, rolled up and fell into the hole. It WAS A 420 YARD HOLE IN ONE!
St. Peter was astonished. He looked at the Lord and asked, "Why did you let him do that?"

The Lord smiled and replied, "Who's he going to tell?"

JOKE 66

Skippy the Dog

A woman goes to her boyfriend's parents' house for Thanksgiving dinner.

This is to be her first time meeting the family and she is very nervous. They all sit down and begin eating a fine meal.

The woman is beginning to feel a little discomfort, thanks to her nervousness and the broccoli casserole. The gas pains are almost making her eyes water. Left with no other choice, she decides to relieve herself a bit and lets out a dainty fart.

It wasn't loud, but everyone at the table heard the poof. Before she even had a chance to be embarrassed, her boyfriend's father looked over at the dog that had been snoozing under the woman's chair, and said in a rather stern voice, "Skippy!".

The woman thought, "This is great!" and a big smile came across her face. A couple of minutes later, she was beginning to feel the pain again. This time, she didn't even hesitate. She let a much louder and longer rrrrrip.

The father again looked at the dog and yelled, "Dammit Skippy!" Once again the woman smiled and thought "Yes!" A few minutes later the woman had to let another rip. This time she didn't even think about it. She let a fart rip that rivaled a train whistle blowing.

Once again, the father looked at the dog with disgust and yelled, "Dammit Skippy, get away from her, before she craps on you!"

JOKE 67

A Rabbit In His Mouth

So I get home this morning and my dog is laying on my porch covered in snow and mud and has a rabbit in his mouth. He's not bloody, just dirty.

Now, my neighbors raised these rabbits for 4H and have blue ribbon winners. I instantly knew it was one of theirs. So I get the rabbit away from my dog, I take it inside, wash all the dirt off and before my neighbors got home I took it over, put him back in the cage and went back home.

Not 30 minutes later I hear my neighbors screaming, so I go out and ask them what's wrong?

They tell me their rabbit died three days ago and they buried it but now it's back in the cage.

JOKE 68 Chocolate Chip Cookies for Me?

An old man was laying on his death bed. He had only hours to live when he suddenly smelled chocolate chip cookies.

He loved chocolate chip cookies more than anything else in the world.

With his last bit of energy, he pulled himself out of bed, across the floor, and to the stairs. Then down the stairs and into the kitchen.

There his wife was baking chocolate chip cookies. As he reached for one, he got smacked across the back of his hand by the wooden spoon his wife was holding.

"Leave them alone!" she said, "They're for the funeral!"

JOKE 69

The Troubled Man

There's a man sitting at a bar just looking at his drink. He stay like that for half an hour. Then, a big trouble-making truck drive steps next to him, takes the drink from the guy, and just drink it all down.

The poor man starts crying. The truck driver says, "Come o man, I was just joking. Here, I'll buy you another drink. I jus can't stand seeing a man crying."

"No, it's not that. This day is the worst of my life. First, I fa asleep, and I'm late to my office. My boss, in an outrage, fire me. When I leave the building to my car, I found out it wa stolen. The police say they can do nothing. I get a cab to retur home and when I leave it, I remember I left my wallet and credi cards there. The cab driver just drives away. I go home an when I get there, I find my wife sleeping with the gardener. leave home and come to this bar. And when I was thinkin about putting an end to my life, you show up and drink m poison."

JOKE 70

Why Are You Crying?

An old man of ninety was sitting on a park bench crying. A policeman noticed this and asked him why he was crying.

"Well," says the old fellow, "I just got married to a twenty-five year old woman. Every morning she makes me a wonderful breakfast, and we have then have fun together laughing and relaxing. In the afternoon she makes me a wonderful lunch and then we make fun together laughing and relaxing again. At dinner time she makes me a wonderful supper and then we relax more and enjoy ourselves."

The policeman looks at the old man and says, "You shouldn't be crying! You should be the happiest man in the world!"

"I know!" says the old man, "I'm crying because I don't remember where I live!"

JOKE 71 Slow Moving Traffic To The Righ

A woman was driving her old beat up car on the highway with her 7 year old son.

She tried to keep up with traffic but they were flying by her. After getting caught in a large group of cars flying down the road, she looked at her speedometer to see she was doing 15 miles over the speed limit.

Slowing down, she moved over to the side and got out of the clump that soon left her behind.

She looked up and saw the flashing lights of a police car.

Pulling over she waited for the officer to come up to her car. As he did he said, "Ma'am do you know why I pulled you over?" Her son piped up from the back seat, "I do... because you couldn't catch the other cars!"

JOKE 72

First Time Confessions

The new priest is nervous about hearing confessions for the first time, so he asks an older priest to sit in on his sessions.

The new priest hears a couple confessions, then the old priest asks him to step out of the confessional for a few suggestions.

The old priest suggests, "Cross you arms over your chest, and rub your chin with one hand."

The new priest tries this.

The old priest suggests, "Try saying things like, 'I see,' 'yes, go on,' and 'I understand.' 'How did you feel about that?'"

The new priest says those things.

The old priest says, "Now, don't you think that's a little better than slapping your knee and saying, 'Oh crap!! What happened next?'"

JOKE 73

The Burglars Plight

My wife has not spoken to me in three days. I think it has something to do with what happened on Sunday night when she thought she heard a noise downstairs.

She nudged me and whispered, "Wake up, wake up!"

"What's the matter?" I asked.

"There are burglars in the kitchen. I think they're eating the tuna casserole I made tonight."

"That'll teach them!" I replied.

JOKE 74

The New Fishing Pole

One day a lady went into a fishing shop to buy her husband a fishing pole for his birthday. She picked up a really nice looking pole and asked the salesman how much it was.

The salesman said, "I am blind but if you give me the pole I can tell how much it is by the weight."

So the lady gave him the pole and he said, "That pole is worth $45." She was amazed at how cheap that was so she picked up another really nice pole, handed it to the man and he said, "This pole is worth $55." She decided that was still less than she wanted to spend so she picked up the nicest looking pole in the place and handed it to the man. "This pole is our best and it is $70." The woman was happy with his response and said she was taking it.

As she was getting the fishing pole rung up, she had to fart really really badly. She thought about it and decided, since the man was blind, there was no way he would know if it was her, or another customer, so she let it all out.

All of a sudden the man says, "It all comes up to $80."

Confused the lady says to him, "But you said the fishing pole was only $70."

He said, "It is. Its $70 for the fishing pole and $10 for the duck call."

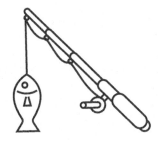

JOKE 75

A Father's Labor Pains

A married couple went to the hospital to have their baby delivered. Upon their arrival, the doctor said he had invented a new machine that would transfer a portion of the mother's pain to the baby's father. He asked if they were willing to try it out and they were both very much in favor of it.

The doctor set the pain transfer to 10%, for starters, explaining that even 10% was probably more pain the father had ever experienced before. However, as the labor progressed, the husband felt fine and asked the doctor to go ahead and "kick it up a notch."

The doctor then adjusted the machine to 20% pain transfer. The husband was still feeling fine. The doctor checked the husband's blood pressure and was amazed at how well he was doing at this point, they decided to try for 50% and the husband continued to feel quite well.

Since the pain transfer was obviously helping out the wife considerably, the husband encouraged the doctor to transfer ALL the pain to him. The wife delivered a healthy baby boy with virtually no pain. She and her husband were ecstatic. When they got home, the mail man was dead on the porch.

JOKE 76

At The Pearly Gates

A woman dies and comes to the Pearly Gates where she tells St. Peter that she would like to find her husband who died a few years ago. She gives him her husband's brief description and name.

St. Peter thinks about it, looks for the name in the book, but he can't find it. He asks the woman to give more detail.

The woman starts: "Well, we've been married for 55 years..."
St. Peter stops her right there and exclaims: "You should have said that first. I need to look in the Book of Martyrs."

JOKE 77

Two great white sharks swimming in the ocean spied a group of people playing too far from the shore.

"Follow me son" the father shark said to the son shark and they swam to the group.

"First we swim around them a few times with just the tip of our fins showing." And they did.

"Well done, son! Now we swim around them a few times with all of our fins showing." And they did.

"Now we eat everybody." And they did.

When they were both gorged, the son asked, "Dad, why didn't we just eat them all at first? Why did we swim around and around them?"

His wise father replied, "Because they taste better if you scare the crap out of them first!"

JOKE 78

Tired of My Wife

A guy was tired of his marriage, so he took out a million dollar policy on his wife with himself as the beneficiary. He then asked around and found a guy who could take care of things. The man introduced himself as "Artie" and said it would cost $50,000 to take out the wife. The husband agreed, but it would come out of the insurance money. Artie said he would need something as a deposit. The husband opened his wallet and all he had was a dollar. Artie grimaced, but accepted it as a down payment.

The next day, Artie followed the wife. When she went into the grocery store, Artie looked around and saw the parking lot was almost empty, so he decided that it was as good a time as any. He followed her to the produce section, crept up behind her, and strangled her.

Unfortunately, the manager walked by and saw this, so Artie had to strangle him too. Meanwhile, the cameras saw all of this, so the security guard called the police. They got there as Artie was walking out, so they cuffed him, and later he confessed to everything. The headline in the paper read:

Artie Chokes Two for a Dollar At Jewel

JOKE 79

Please Save My Duck!

A woman brings a very limp duck into a veterinary surgeon.

As she lays her beloved pet duck on the table, the vet puts his stethoscope to the bird's chest and listens carefully.

A moment later the vet shakes his head and says sadly, "I'm really sorry mam, but your duck, Cuddles, has passed away."

The woman becomes quite distressed and begins to cry.

"Are you sure?" she says with tears flooding from her eyes.

"Yes mam, I am sure" the vet responds. "Your duck is definitely dead."

"But how can you be so sure?" the woman protests. "I mean, you haven't done any testing on him or anything have you? Perhaps he's just stunned or in a coma or something."

The vet rolls his eyes, then turns around and leaves the room.

A few minutes later he returns with a black Labrador retriever.

As the duck's owner looks on in amazement, the Labrador stands on his hind legs, puts his front paws on the examination table and sniffs around the duck from top to bottom. He then looks up at the vet with sad eyes and shakes his head.

The vet pats the dog on the head and takes it out of the room.

A few minutes later the vet returns with a cat. The cat jumps on the table and delicately sniffs at the bird from its head to its feet. After a moment the cat looks up, shakes its head, meows softly and strolls out of the room. The vet looks at the woman and says, "Look mam I'm really sorry, but as I said before, this is most definitely a duck that is no longer of this world. Your duck is dead."

The vet then turns to his computer terminal, hits a few keys and produces a bill, which he hands to the woman.

The duck's owner, still in shock, looks at the bill and sees it is $150.

"$150 just to tell me my duck is dead!" she shrieks with incredulity

The vet shrugs his shoulders and says, "I'm sorry mam. If you'd taken my word for it, the bill would have been $20. However, with the Lab Report and the Cat Scan, it's now $150."

The Woods Report

JOKE 80

Tender Tony

Ethel was traveling alone and she was a bit lonely in the hotel all on her own. She thought, "I'll call one of those men you see advertised in phone books for escorts and sex and have some fun."

She looked through the phone book, found a full page ad for a guy calling himself Tender Tony – a very handsome man with assorted physical skills flexing in the photo. He had all the right muscles in all the right places, thick wavy hair, long powerful legs, dazzling smile, six pack abs and she felt quite certain she could bounce a sixpence off his well-oiled bum. She figured, "What the heck, nobody will ever know. I'll give him a call."

After a short ring, there was a response, "Good evening, ma'am, how may I help you?" Oh my, he sounded sooo sexy!

Afraid she would lose her nerve if she hesitated, she rushed right in, "Hi, I hear you give a great massage. I'd like you to come to my hotel room and give me one. No, wait, I should be straight with you. I'm in town all alone and what I really want to make love. I want it hot, and I want it now. Bring implements, toys, rubber, leather, whips, everything you've got in your bag of tricks. We'll go hot and heavy all night – tie me up, cover me in chocolate syrup and whipped cream, anything and everything!!! Now how does that sound?"

The male voice responded, "That sounds absolutely fantastic madam, but you need to press 9 for an outside line."

JOKE 81

Forrest Gump Goes to Heave[n]

Forrest Gump died and went to heaven. When he got to the Pearly Gates Saint Peter told him that new rules were in effect due to the advances in education on earth. In order to gain admittance a prospective Heavenly Soul must answer three questions:

1. Name two days of the week that begin with T.

2. How many seconds are in a year?

3. What is God's first name?

Forrest thought for a few minutes and answered, 1. The two days of the week that begin with T are Today and Tomorrow 2. There are 12 seconds in a year. 3. God has two-first names and they are Andy and Howard."

Saint Peter said, "OK I'll buy Today and Tomorrow, even though it's not the answer I expected, your answer is acceptable. But how did you get 12 seconds in a year and why did you ever think that God's first name was either Andy or Howard?"

Forrest responded, "Well, January 2nd, February 2nd, March 2nd,..."

"OK, I give in" said Saint Peter, but what about the God's first name stuff?

Forrest said, "Well, from the song... Andy walks with me, Andy talks with me, Andy tells me I am his own... and the prayer... Our Father which Art in Heaven, Howard be thy name...."

Saint Peter let him in without further ado!

JOKE 82   The Blind Man Parachuting

man was driving and saw a truck stalled on the side of the highway
hat had ten penguins standing next to it. The man pulled over and
sked the truck driver if he needed any help. The truck driver replied,
f you can take these penguins to the zoo while I wait for AAA that
ill be great!" The man agreed and the penguins hopped into the
ack of his car. Two hours later, the trucker was back on the road
gain and decided to check on the penguins. He showed up at the zoo
nd they weren't there! He headed back into his truck and started
riving around the town, looking for any sign of the penguins, the
an, or his car. While driving past a movie theater, the truck driver
potted the guy walking out with the ten penguins. The truck driver
elled, "What are you doing? You were supposed to take them to the
oo!" The man replied, "I did and then I had some extra money so I
ok them to go see a movie."

JOKE 83

The Lie Detector Robot

A man buys a lie detector robot that slaps people who lie. He decides to test it at dinner. He asks his son, "Son, where were you today during school hours?" "At school." The robot slaps the son. "Okay, I went to the movies!" The father asks, "Which one?" "Harry Potter." The robot slaps the son again. "Okay, I was watching a R rated movie!" The father replies, "What? When I was your age I didn't even know what a R rated movie was!" The robot slaps the father. The mom chimes in, "Haha! After all, he is your son!" The robot slaps the mother.

JOKE 84

Is He My Son?

A husband and wife have four boys. The odd part of it is that the older three have red hair, light skin, and are tall, while the youngest son has black hair, dark eyes, and is short. The father eventually takes ill and is lying on his deathbed when he turns to his wife and says, "Honey, before I die, be completely honest with me. Is our youngest son my child?" The wife replies, "I swear on everything that's holy that he is your son." With that, the husband passes away. The wife then mutters, "Thank God he didn't ask about the other three."

JOKE 85

The Chastity Belt

A knight went off to fight in the Holy Crusades but befor leaving he made his wife wear a chastity belt. After tightl securing it to her, he handed the key to his best friend with th instruction: "If I do not return within seven years, unlock m wife and set her free to lead a normal life."

The knight then rode off on the first leg of his journey to th Holy Land, but he had only traveled barely an hour when he wa suddenly aware of the sound of pounding hooves behind him. H turned to see that it was his best friend.

"What is the problem?" asked the knight.

His best friend replied: "You gave me the wrong key."

JOKE 86

Throw It Into The River

A preacher was completing a temperance sermon. With great expression he said, "If I had all the beer in the world, I'd take it and throw it into the river."

With even greater emphasis, his arms in the air, he said, "And if I had all the wine in the world, I'd take it and throw it into the river."

And then finally, with a raised voice he finished, "And if I had all the whiskey in the world, I'd take it and throw it into the river." He sat down and revered silence filled the church.

O'Malley, the song leader who dozed off during the sermon, stood up very cautiously and announced with a smile, "For our closing song, let us sing Hymn #365: "Shall We Gather at the River."

JOKE 87

The Old Maid

In a tiny village lived an old maid. In spite of her old age, she was still a virgin. She was very proud of it. She knew her last days were getting closer, so she told the local undertaker that she wanted the following inscription on her tombstone: "Born as a virgin, lived as a virgin, died as a virgin."

Not long after, the old maid died peacefully, and the undertaker told his men what the lady had said. The men went to carve it in, but the lazy no-goods they were, they thought the inscription to be unnecessarily long. They simply wrote: "Returned unopened."

The Taxi Driver

We were dressed and ready to go out for a dinner & theatre that evening we turned on a night light, turned the answering machine on, covered our pet budgie and put the cat in the backyard. We phoned the local Taxi company and requested a taxi.

The taxi arrived and we opened the front door to leave the house. As we walked out the door, the cat we had put out in the yard scooted back into the house. We didn't want the cat shut in the house because he always tries to get at the budgie. My wife walked on out to the taxi, while I went back inside to get the cat. The cat ran upstairs, with me in hot pursuit.

Waiting in the cab, my wife didn't want the driver to know that the house will be empty for the night. So, she explained to the taxi driver that I would be out soon. "He is just going upstairs to say goodbye to my mother."

A few minutes later, I got into the cab. "Sorry I took so long," I said, as we drove away. "That stupid witch was hiding under the bed. I had poke her with a coat hanger to get her to come out! She tried to take off, so I grabbed her by the neck. Then, I had to wrap her in a blanket to keep her from scratching me and it worked! I hauled her fat butt downstairs and threw her out into the back yard! She'd better not crap in the vegetable garden again!"

The silence in the Taxi was deafening.

JOKE 89

Pay With A Kiss

Walking up to a department store's fabric counter, a pretty girl asked, "I want to buy this material for a new dress. How much does it cost?"

"Only one kiss per yard, " replied the smirking male clerk.

"That's fine," replied the girl. "I'll take ten yards."

With expectation and anticipation written all over his face, the clerk hurriedly measured out and wrapped the cloth, then held it out teasingly.

The girl snapped up the package and pointed to a little old man standing beside her. "Grandpa will pay the bill," she smiled.

The Zipped Skirt

downtown Roanoke, at a crowded bus stop, an attractive girl was aiting for a bus. She was decked out in a tight leather mini skirt ith matching tight leather boots and jacket. As the bus rolled up and became her turn to get on, she became aware that her skirt was o tight to allow her leg to come up to the height of the first step on e bus.

ightly embarrassed and with a quick smile to the bus driver she ached behind her and unzipped her skirt a little thinking that this ould give her enough slack to raise her leg. Again she tried to make e step onto the bus only to discover she still couldn't!

o, a little more embarrassed she once again reached behind her and zipped her skirt a little more and for a second time attempted the ep and once again, much to her chagrin she could not raise her leg cause of the tight skirt.

o, with a coy little smile to the driver she again unzipped the fending skirt to give a little more slack and again was unable to ake the step.

bout this time a big burly man that was behind her in the line picked r up easily from the waist and placed her lightly on the step of the us. Well, she went ballistic and turned to the would-be hero reeching at him "How dare you touch me!! I don't even know who u are!"

t this, the big guy drawled, "Well ma'am normally I would agree with u but after you unzipped my fly three times, I kinda figured it would OK!"

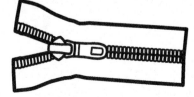

JOKE 91

Billy Bob's Obituary

A woman from the deepest South goes into the local newspaper office to see that the obituary for her recently deceased husband is written. The obit editor informs her that the fee for the obituary is 50 cents a word.

She pauses, reflects and then says, "Well, then, let it read, 'Billy Bob died'."

Amused at the woman's thrift, the editor says, "Sorry ma'am, there is a 7 word minimum on all obituaries."

Only a little flustered, she thinks things over and in a few seconds says, "In that case, let it read, 'Billy Bob died – 1983 truck for sale.'"

Horseback Riding Experience

A blonde decides to try horseback riding, even though she has had no lessons, nor prior experience. She mounts the horse unassisted, and the horse immediately springs into motion.

It gallops along at a steady and rhythmic pace, but the blonde begins to slide from the saddle. In terror, she grabs for the horse's mane, but cannot seem to get a firm grip. She tries to throw her arms around the horse's neck, but she slides down the horse's side anyway. The horse gallops along, seemingly impervious to its slipping rider.

Finally, giving up her frail grip, the blonde attempts to leap away from the horse and throw herself to safety. Unfortunately, her foot has become entangled in the stirrup, she is now at the mercy of the horse's pounding hooves as her head is struck against the ground over and over.

As her head is battered against the ground, she is mere moments away from unconsciousness when to her great fortune Frank, the Walmart greeter, sees her dilemma and unplugs the horse.

JOKE 93

$50 Helicopter Ride

Morris and his wife Esther went to the state fair every year, an
every year Morris would say, "Esther, I'd like to ride in tha
helicopter." Esther always replied, "I know Morris, but tha
helicopter ride is fifty dollars, and fifty dollars is fifty dollars."

One year, Esther and Morris went to the fair, and Morris said
"Esther, I'm 85 years old. If I don't ride that helicopter today,
might never get another chance." To this, Esther replie
"Morris that helicopter ride is fifty dollars, and fifty dollars i
fifty dollars."

The pilot overheard the couple and said, "Folks, I'll make you
deal. I'll take the both of you for a ride. If you can stay quiet fo
the entire ride and don't say a word I won't charge you a penny
But if you say one word it's fifty dollars."

Morris and Esther agreed and up they went. The pilot did al
kinds of fancy maneuvers, but not a word was heard. He did hi
daredevil tricks over and over again, but still not a word. Whe
they landed, the pilot turned to Morris and said, "By golly, I di
everything I could to get you to yell out, but you didn't. I'
impressed!"

Morris replied, "Well, to tell you the truth, I almost sai
something when Esther fell out, but you know, fifty dollars i
fifty dollars!"

JOKE 94

The Baseball Bat Attack

A wife comes home late one night, arriving a day early from being out of town. She quietly enters the house and goes straight to the bedroom. From under the blanket she sees four legs instead of two. She reaches for a baseball bat and starts hitting the blanket as hard as she can.

Once she's done, she goes to the kitchen to have a drink. As she enters, she sees her husband there, reading a magazine.

"Hi, Darling", he says, "Your parents have come to visit us, so I let them stay in our bedroom."

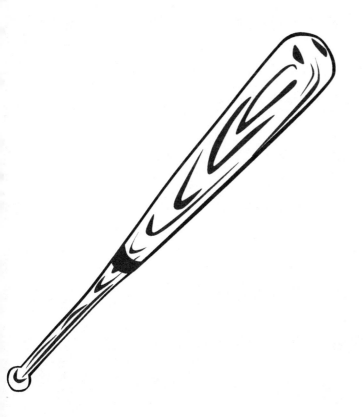

JOKE 95

Gang of Bikers

A young man appeared before St. Peter at the Pearly Gates.

"Have you ever done anything of particular merit?" St. Peter asked.

"Well, I can think of one thing," the young man replied

"On a trip to the Black Hills out in South Dakota, I came upon a gang of bikers who were threatening a young woman. I directed them to leave her alone, but they wouldn't listen. So, I approached the largest and most tattooed biker and smacked him in the face, kicked his bike over, ripped out his nose ring, and threw it on the ground. I yelled, "Now, back off or I'll kick the crap out of all of you!""

St. Peter was impressed, "When did this happen?"

"Couple of minutes ago."

Help...I need My Car Keys!

When my husband and I arrived at an automobile dealership to pick up our car, we were told the keys had been locked in it.

We went to the service department and found a blonde mechanic working feverishly to unlock the driver's side door. As I watched from the passenger side, I instinctively tried the door handle and discovered that it was unlocked.

"Hey," I announced to the technician, "it's open!"

To which he replied, "I know — I already got that side."

JOKE 97

How Do You Say "Lafayette"

A honeymooning couple was passing through Louisiana. When they were approaching Lafayette, they started arguing about the pronunciation of the town. They argued back and forth until they got to the town, where they decided to stop for lunch.

As they stood at the counter, the man said, "Before we order, could you please settle an argument for us. Would you very slowly pronounce where we are."

The guy behind the corner leaned over and said, "Burrrrrrrr gerrrrrr Kiiiiing"

JOKE 98   The Elderly Farmer

Ron, an elderly man in Florida, has owned a large farm for several years. He had a large pond in the back. It was properly shaped for swimming, so he fixed it up nice with picnic tables, horseshoe courts and some orange and lime trees.

One evening, the old farmer decided to go down to the pond, as he hadn't been there for a while, and look it over. He grabbed a five gallon bucket to bring back some fruit.

As he neared the pond, he heard voices shouting and laughing with glee. When he came closer, he saw it was a bunch of young women skinny dipping in his pond. He made the women aware of his presence, and they all went to the deep end.

One of the women shouted to him, "We're not coming out until you leave!"

Ron frowned, "I didn't come down here to watch you ladies swim naked or make you get out of the pond." Holding the bucket up Ron said, "I'm here to feed the alligator."

JOKE 99

The 10 Commandments

A Sunday school teacher was discussing the Ten Commandments with her five and six year olds.

After explaining the commandment to "honor" thy Father and thy Mother, she asked, "Is there a commandment that teaches us how to treat our brothers and sisters?"

Without missing a beat one little boy, the oldest of a family, answered, "Thou shall not kill."

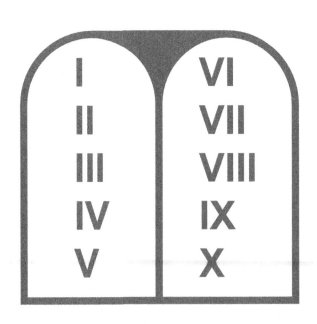

Four Catholic Ladies

Four Catholic ladies are having coffee together. The first one tells her friends, "My son is a priest. When he walks into a room, everyone calls him 'Father'."

The second woman chirps, "My son is a Bishop. Whenever he walks into a room, people say, 'Your Grace'."

The third woman says smugly, "My son is a Cardinal. Whenever he walks into a room, people say, 'Your Eminence'."

The fourth woman sips her coffee in silence. The first three women give her this subtle "Well.....?"

She replies, "My son is a gorgeous, 6'2", hard bodied stripper. When he walks into a room, people say, 'Oh my God!!!'"

Printed in Great Britain
by Amazon